A FISHERMAN'S TALE

by Keith Faulkner and
Jonathan Lambert

PROSPERO
B·O·O·K·S
A DIVISION OF CHAPTERS INC.

Sam is fishing in a rock pool.
What is he going to find?

Sam's caught something! It's a tiny...

Sam puts the fish in a jar,

but when he gets home the fish has grown...

Sam moves the fish to a tank,

but the fish grows even...

Sam carries the fish to the bath,

but the fish grows still ...

Sam wheels the fish back to the sea

'My goodness!' says Sam ...

and it grows and grows until …

'You're a **WHALE!**'

Sam's new friend is a goldfish,